EAGLES OF AMERICA

DOROTHY HINSHAW PATENT

photographs by
WILLIAM MUÑOZ

Holiday House/New York

The author and photographer wish to thank the following people and institutions for their help with this book: Ken and Jody Wolff, Kate Davis, Judy Hoy, Carlos Rodriquez, Busch Gardens, Lowry Park Zoo, and Northwest Trek.

A portion of the royalties from this book are being donated to the Grounded Eagle Foundation, Inc., HCR 31, Box 900, Condon, MT 59826-9706.

Text copyright © 1995 by Dorothy Hinshaw Patent
Photographs copyright © 1995 by William Muñoz
Printed in the United States of America
First Edition
Library of Congress Cataloging-in-Publication Data
Patent, Dorothy Hinshaw.
Eagles of America / Dorothy Hinshaw Patent ; photographs by
William Muñoz. — 1st ed.
p.   cm.
Includes index.
ISBN 0-8234-1198-2 (hardcover)
1. Bald eagle—North America—Juvenile literature.   2. Golden
eagle—North America—Juvenile literature.   [1. Bald eagle.
2. Golden eagle.   3. Eagles.]   I. Muñoz, William, ill.   II. Title.
QL696.F32P36   1995   95-6083   CIP   AC

Contents

A bald eagle in flight.

CHAPTER ONE

What Is an Eagle?

Eagles are among the biggest birds that fly. There are sixty-six kinds of eagles. They live on every continent except Antarctica.

North America is home to two kinds of eagles: the bald eagle and the golden eagle. Both of them are very large. The bald eagle's wings can spread out to 8 feet (2.4 meters). The golden eagle's are almost as big. The bald eagle is our national bird. Its image appears on the national seal.

The bald eagle was placed on the national seal of the United States of America in 1782.

An eagle's talons allow it to grip tightly. *The hooked beak of an eagle helps it feed on its prey.*

Eagles are powerful hunters, or predators. They are close relatives of hawks. Their feet are armed with sharp, curved claws, called talons, for grabbing onto their food, or prey. Their strong beaks have a hook at the end for tearing at meat. Some eagles, including both balds and goldens, also feed on animals that are already dead, called carrion. Bald eagles are more likely to eat carrion than goldens. In Alaska, where bald eagles are common, they often feed at garbage dumps. Because they feed on dead animals, eagles are sometimes blamed by ranchers for killing livestock. But in fact, the livestock are already dead. Eagles only rarely kill domesticated animals such as very small newborn lambs.

Eagles find their food with their amazing eyes. They can see a mouse moving in the grass a mile away or a rabbit at a distance of two miles. An eagle's eyes are at the front of its head, like ours. But it can see eight times as well as we can.

The eyes of an eagle face forward, giving it excellent vision.

Eagles use their broad wings to soar on the wind for long periods of time. They take advantage of warm air rising along the edges of mountains and hills to float without effort. As an eagle soars, it looks for possible prey. When it spots something to eat, it folds its wings and dives downward. A golden eagle can reach a speed of 180 miles (288 kilometers) per hour or even faster. Adult eagles can judge perfectly when to open their talons. As the eagle hits its target, the talons close tightly around the prey, and the eagle carries its food to a nearby branch to feed.

Eagles also have a good sense of hearing. But their sense of smell is poor.

If young eagles don't die before they are old enough to breed, they can live to be quite old. They might live at least into their twenties if they're not killed by humans first. In captivity, both kinds of American eagles have lived to be close to fifty years old.

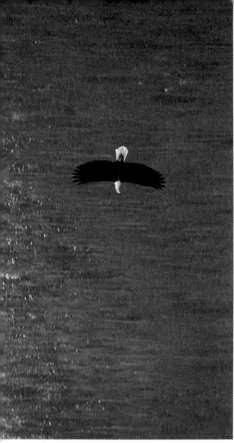

A bald eagle soars on the wind, looking for prey.

It reaches forward with its talons to capture a fish.

It grabs the fish from the surface of the water.

9

The red-tailed hawk (left) is a close relative of the golden eagle (right).

CHAPTER TWO

Our Two Eagles

The bald and golden are both called eagles, but they are not really close relatives. Bald eagles (which scientists call *Haliaeetus leucocephalus*) are more closely related to European vultures than they are to golden eagles. Golden eagles, whose scientific name is *Aquila chrysaetos,* are more similar to red-tailed hawks. Males of both kinds typically weigh 8 to 9½ pounds (3.6 to 4.3 kilograms). Females are larger than males, weighing up to 13 pounds (5.9 kilograms). A rare female is even bigger.

The mature bald eagle has white head feathers, a yellow beak, and yellow eyes.

It is easy to tell adult eagles apart. By the age of five or six, the bald eagle has a snowy white head and tail. It probably got its name in the seventeenth century. English settlers referred to the birds as "balde," the English and Welsh word for white. The rest of its feathers are blackish brown. Its eyes, beak, legs, and feet are yellow.

An adult golden eagle has dark brown feathers covering most of its body. The feathers over its head and neck are golden brown, the source of its name. Its tail has gray bands, one wide and one narrow in females, and a number of narrow bands in males. Its beak is darker in color than a bald eagle's beak. Its eyes are brown.

An adult golden eagle has light brown feathers on the back of its neck, brown eyes, and a horn-colored beak.

The lower legs of a golden eagle are covered with fine feathers.

Young bald and golden eagles are difficult to recognize by anyone but an expert. Only one trait is always helpful in telling the two apart—at any age a golden eagle has feathers covering its legs, while a bald eagle's lower legs are bare. As young birds, both have mostly brown feathers and brown eyes. Immature goldens have white tails with a broad, black band at the tip. As they grow older, the white decreases. Young birds of both kinds have some white on the body and have brown eyes. At around the age of three or four, a young bald eagle begins to develop adult traits.

The feathers on the head of a three- or four-year-old bald eagle are not completely white.

Eagles and other birds shed their old feathers at least once a year. This process is called molting. Some birds lose their feathers over a short period of time. But eagles lose them very gradually. They need enough wing feathers at all times for soaring in order to find food.

Birds keep their feathers clean by bathing and preening. When a bird preens its feathers, it uses its beak and feet to smooth them. It also coats them with oil from a gland near the base of its tail.

Bald eagle chicks have soft gray down feathers that they outgrow rapidly. (Photo courtesy of Will Krynen)

A young bald eagle eats a dead fish it dragged from the water.

Fish is the favorite food of bald eagles. The birds have tiny spines on the bottoms of their feet that help hold onto their slippery prey. Bald eagles also eat water birds like ducks and gulls, and small mammals such as rabbits.

Golden eagles feed mostly on rabbits and mice. They eat birds like grouse, too.

Both kinds of American eagles mate for life. But if one bird dies, the other finds a new mate. Eagles may court their mate by flying in a wavy pattern. Bald eagle pairs may lock their talons in flight and tumble downward together.

Eagles use the same nest each year and add onto it every season. A nest used for many years may be 20 feet (6 meters) deep and can weigh 2 tons (over 1800 kilograms). Bald eagle nests are usually in big trees. But in the Far North, where there are no trees, the birds build their nests on high parts of the land. The nest site is always near the water, so the eagles can be close to their fish prey.

Golden eagles usually build their nests on cliffs, but in some areas, they prefer trees.

This freshly built bald eagle nest is smaller than a nest that has been used for many years.

Eagles normally lay two eggs a few days apart, but sometimes they lay three. An eagle egg is about the same size as a chicken egg, only more rounded in shape. Golden eagles hatch after about forty-three days. Bald eagle eggs hatch in around thirty-five days. The female usually sits on the nest to keep the eggs warm, and the male feeds her. Both parents take care of the young. They bring food to the nest, tear off small pieces, and carefully feed it to their hungry youngsters.

A parent bald eagle watches over its offspring,
which are almost old enough to fly.

Two young bald eagles with one of their parents in a tree.

Because one egg is laid a few days earlier, it also hatches earlier. When there isn't enough food for more than one eaglet, the oldest, which is larger, gets most of the food. The other eaglet dies, either by starving or because it is killed by its stronger sibling. This is more likely to happen in goldens. However, sometimes three eaglets survive in one nest if there is plenty to eat. Eaglets can fly ten to twelve weeks after hatching. Then they must learn the difficult skill of hunting. Until the fall migration, however, the eaglets may still be fed at least partly by their parents.

A young bald eagle about to land.

Some bald eagles living in the North spend the winter in the Rush Valley in Utah. Others travel as far south as the California–Nevada border, while some remain in northern states like Montana. Southern bald eagles travel northward for the winter. Some golden eagles do not migrate, while others do.

Many bald eagles, like this one, spend the winter in Montana.

CHAPTER THREE

Once Abundant Eagles

Both bald and golden eagles used to be common in North America. Bald eagles once lived across all of Canada and in every state except Hawaii. During the nineteenth and twentieth centuries, many bald eagles died. The species disappeared over much of its range and became officially endangered in the lower forty-eight states.

Glacier National Park in Montana provides perfect bald eagle habitat.

A golden eagle flies across a Montana meadow.

The golden eagle inhabited most of western North America. It also was found across the northern areas of the world, mainly in the mountains and hilly areas with open spaces where it could hunt. The golden eagle lived in smaller numbers in the eastern United States as far south as North Carolina and Tennessee. Now, golden eagles are rarely seen there and are endangered in many parts of Europe.

The loss of so many eagles has occurred for many reasons. People have taken over wildlands for highways, shopping malls, and vacation homes. The huge nests of bald eagles require large trees. Much old-growth forest where such trees are found has been cut down for timber.

For many years, the chemical DDT was used in the United States to kill insect pests. Then scientists found that DDT collected in the bodies of birds like eagles through the food chain. An eagle with too much DDT in her body laid eggs with very thin shells. The thin shells cracked easily, killing the embryo inside before it could hatch. Bald eagles and other fish-eating birds were especially sensitive to DDT. Once it was clear how dangerous DDT was to birds, it was banned in the United States. After a few years, bald eagles again laid eggs with strong shells. But meanwhile, bald eagle populations had declined.

Injured captive golden eagle.

Both bald and golden eagles die from a number of other causes. Sometimes they get caught in traps set for fur-bearing animals. They run into power lines and are electrocuted. Even though killing eagles is a federal crime, some people shoot or poison eagles because they think the birds attack domesticated animals. In the late 1980s, thousands of golden eagles were poisoned in the state of Wyoming alone.

Eagles are also killed for their feathers, which people value enough to pay fifty dollars or more for just one feather. Eagle feathers are important in many Native American ceremonies. When eagles die, the bodies are supposed to be turned over to the government. Indian tribes apply to the government to receive the feathers for tribal use. Eagles are honored by Native Americans because of their great size and strength. To tribes like the Oglala Sioux, eagles are the most powerful of all birds.

War chief John Peter Paul of the Confederated Salish and Kootenai tribes dances wearing an eagle feather headdress and carrying an eagle feather fan at a summer celebration.

Bald eagles are becoming more common in states like Montana.

There's good news for bald eagles today. Because it was endangered, the bald eagle received a great deal of attention from scientists and conservationists. People worked hard to help increase bald eagle populations. In 1963, only 417 pairs of bald eagles nested in all the lower forty-eight states. Now, there are more than 3,000 nesting pairs, some in each state. Because it has recovered so well, the bald eagle has been removed from the endangered species list in all of the lower forty-eight states except Arizona, New Mexico, and parts of California, Oklahoma, and Texas. It is now called a "threatened species." Golden eagles are being helped, too. They are being reintroduced into areas of the eastern states where they used to live.

CHAPTER FOUR

Helping Eagles Survive

Humans bring on problems for wild animals in the modern world. But many people care about the welfare of birds like eagles. Some care enough to devote their lives to helping them. They believe that because we injure and kill wild things, we must also help them heal when we can. Here is a typical eagle rescue story.

A young bald eagle lands on a dead deer on the roadside of Highway 83 in northwestern Montana. The bird feeds eagerly, filling its stomach with the energy-rich meat. Only a few weeks ago, the eagle's parents were feeding it, but now it is on its own. Learning to plunge down from high in the air to the water or ground to grab a fish or rabbit takes practice. Young eagles make plenty of mistakes as they learn to hunt. When they get hungry, they are more than willing to feed on food that is already dead, like road-kill deer.

If a deer carcass like this one is close to a road, young bald eagles that feed on it can be hit by cars when they try to fly.

After eating so much, the bird is heavy and has trouble taking off. It uses the tree-lined road as a runway, starting off low and gaining altitude as it gains speed. But it doesn't get high fast enough. A pickup truck driving down the road hits the bird with its windshield.

The injured eagle flaps helplessly onto the road. Fortunately for the bird, the driver of the truck knows that just down the road lies The Raptor Room. Raptors are birds, like eagles, that hunt and kill prey. At The Raptor Room, Ken Wolff has a government permit that allows him to take in eagles and other wounded birds. He nurses them back to health when possible. Ken and those like him are called "wildlife rehabilitators."

Ken Wolff sits with Sheba, a blind golden eagle injured by a car. Ken uses Sheba for educational programs, teaching children about raptors.

When Ken gets the bird, he finds it has a broken wing and a probable concussion, a temporary injury to the brain. This young eagle is lucky—its injuries can heal, so it has a good chance of flying freely once more. After surgery, Ken puts the bird into an indoor, heated recovery room where it begins the healing process.

Taking care of an injured eagle is hard work. Eagles are powerful, fearless animals. Their beaks and talons are deadly weapons that can injure those who work to help them, so rehabilitators must be very careful. They need to wear thick leather gloves and keep their faces out of reach of the birds when working with them.

Until its wounds heal, the injured bird stays in a recovery cage. It is fed meat every day. But healing is only the first part of rehabilitation. If an eagle is grounded for even a week, it needs physical therapy to become strong enough to fly again. Once an injured wing is healed and any pins are removed, therapy begins. Ken and his wife, Jody, work with an eagle six to eight times a day. They stretch its wings to keep the joints flexible. During the four to six weeks it takes to heal, the bird loses strength in its flight muscles.

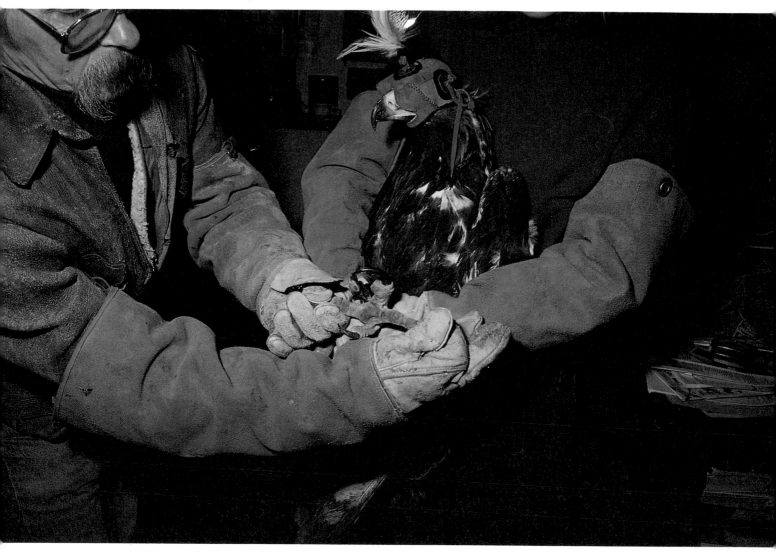

Ken and his wife, Jody, work with an injured golden eagle. The hood over the eagle's head calms it, making physical therapy easier.

Two young bald eagles in The Raptor Room flight pen, where they will regain the strength to fly again.

As soon as possible, the injured bird is placed in an outdoor, unheated recovery cage. As it regains strength, it is moved into the flight pen. The Grounded Eagle Foundation has the largest flight pen in the country for helping birds recover. The room is 120 feet long and has a 160-foot flight path between the perches. Recovering eagles live in the flight pen, where they are encouraged to fly by being chased several times a day. At first, the birds run or flap across the ground. Bit by bit, they become stronger and start flying. A badly injured bird may take months to get off the ground. Once an eagle can fly again, Ken gives it live prey to capture. He must be sure the bird can hunt successfully before releasing it. Otherwise, it could starve to death.

Finally, after weeks or even months, the injured bird is ready for release. Ken takes it to a safe place. The cage is opened, and the bird comes out carefully. Then it takes off, flying low over the ground. Bit by bit, it lifts higher and higher, finally landing in a nearby tree. Ken packs up his truck and heads back to the Grounded Eagle Foundation headquarters. He has work to do, taking care of the eagles, ospreys, hawks, and other birds that depend on him to help them become wild again.

While Jody Wolff looks on, a healed young bald eagle heads back into freedom.

With the aid of people like Ken, we can make it possible for eagles to survive in the crowded modern world. As the populations of eagles increase, so does our own population. This means more pressure on eagles' homes as humans take

38

over more and more wild places. As a result, more eagles will be injured and need to be healed before returning to the wild. One way we can all help is to support wildlife rehabilitators in their work. Simple habits like recycling can help reduce the pollution that endangers plants and animals. We can also back efforts to preserve wildlife habitat around the world so that wild things will always have homes. If enough people care and help, we can all hope to see a beautiful eagle soar overhead, pause, and plunge down like a rocket to capture a healthy meal. It's a sight no one can ever forget.

Sheba, the blind golden eagle, waits patiently on her perch at an educational program.

Index

(italicized numbers indicate photos)